T0030832

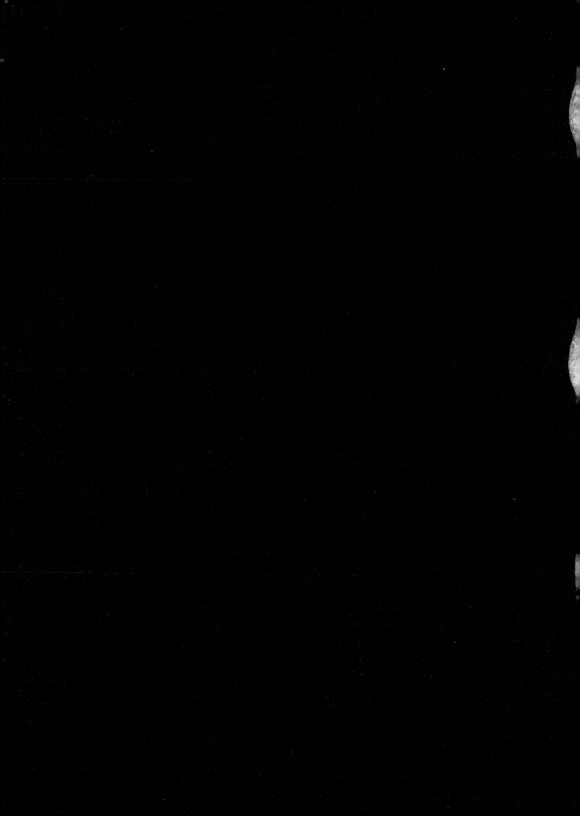

GILLS

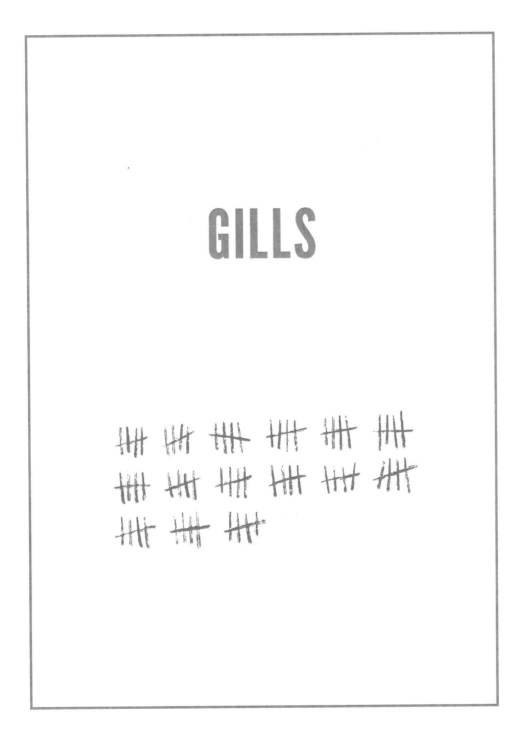

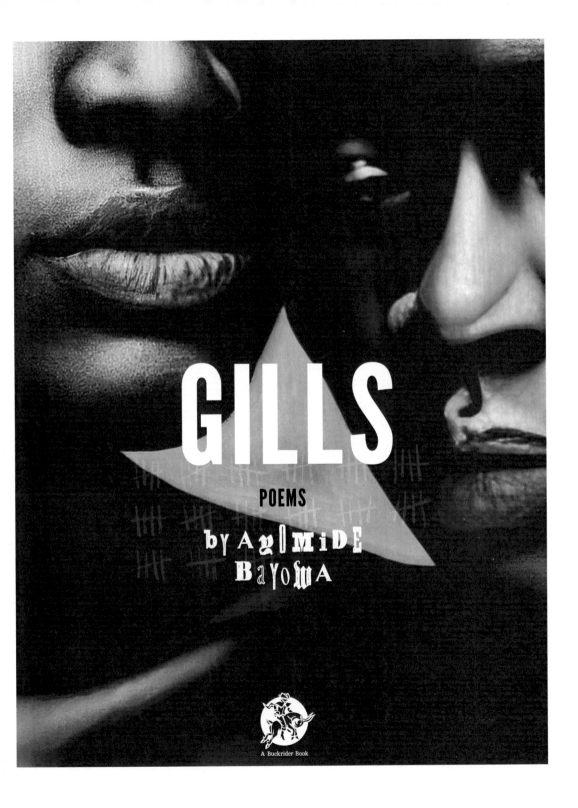

GILLS

POEMS

by AYOMIDE
BAYOWA

A Buckrider Book

© Ayomide Bayowa, 2023

No part of this publication may be reproduced, stored in a retrieval system or transmitted, in any form or by any means, without the prior written consent of the publisher or a license from the Canadian Copyright Licensing Agency (Access Copyright). For an Access Copyright license, visit www.accesscopyright.ca or call toll free to 1-800-893-5777.

Published by Buckrider Books
an imprint of Wolsak and Wynn Publishers
280 James Street North
Hamilton, ON L8R2L3
www.wolsakandwynn.ca

Editor: Paul Vermeersch | Copy editor: Ashley Hisson
Cover and interior design: Kilby Smith-McGregor | Cover image: Emanuel Bustos Orellana
Author photograph: Ayomide Isaac Julius
Typeset in Freight Text Pro, Legue Gothic and Alta California
Printed by Coach House Printing Company, Toronto, Canada

10 9 8 7 6 5 4 3 2 1

The publisher gratefully acknowledges the support of the Ontario Arts Council, the Canada Council for the Arts and the Government of Canada.

Library and Archives Canada Cataloguing in Publication

Title: Gills / by Ayomide Bayowa.
Names: Bayowa, Ayomide, author.
Description: Poems.
Identifiers: Canadiana 20230181775 | ISBN 9781989496657 (softcover)
Classification: LCC PS8603.A9485 G55 2023 | DDC C811/.6—dc23

|||| |||| |||| |||

CoNTentS

|||| |||| |||| |||| |||| ||

DEdiCation.

For Veronica,

> It serves me right to have had a taste
> of your sweetness before the unexpected expiration.
> My mileage is currently over twenty, and I must say –
> I haven't come across a better humanitarian
> that diets her gut to nutrify everyone else's.
> I will return to the soil I threw at your face years
> back with enough white chocolates for the neighbour-
> hood's kids and even grown-ups: like you taught me
> how foreigners act. Just exercise a little bit more patience
> despite the universal suffrage you lived to exercise as if
> a right to suffer on your children for nothing.

> For Akinfolarin Pojo,

>> Quarter to an uneven hour,
>> I wake and oath to reap breath beans
>> as life's broadest breadth scope:
>> a cut cord & backstage pianist's stricken chord
>> a forsaken flow like a Moses's basket deliverable
>> a just found sugar ant in a farmer's cup of tea
>> the only affordable seasonal sickle.
>> Not much goes wrong: many-a-homeland's flag
>> wave the prints of soiled palms –
>> the few surviving farmers are low scale sicklers
>> loyal to the earth & its fullness of dearth
>> thereof. A pastor with tractor-oiled shiny lips
>> groaned by with a bread-crumb life-everlasting
>> sermon of Christ as mere skinny politician.
>> The least trick a dying countryman could pull
>> with a barn of palliative band to entertain no
>> further dying on a deforested rood.

For Serg. Ojeniyi Samson,
As I soak in this mud I originally am,
recreating & sighing upon our last moments together,
May this sorrowful berry your bear departure
leaves behind not take too long before withering.

To be sincere,
as my Oyinbo editor reached out to me, asking
why I wrote this book, I lied and spoke professionally
as if I knew life more than you three.

– Ayòmi

Bills

One time, I was a mermaid
Swept ashore like a blank verse's runoff:
it's a globe show of a life above the water.
ash dumpers. The narrator,
was salted away upstage right to the feet
loonies & more so, a quarter. He wept to
hates him enough to be chased toward &
from wanting to jump in the water; like
afterwards. Who shall remain to log this

& a believer at once.
a sea bin or a loose fin,
Basically, tape dubs of perilous sins or
swamped downstage centre,
of a foreigner with feels coined into toonies,
be taken back home, in quote of that which
beyond the sea. Just as we aren't really free
into the railway track to see what happens
poem in a lifetime's imbalance sheet?

On a scale of five, it's goddamn costly
there's no nearer date to book for baptism.
For why else do I look like the I am
word, as complex as kids staining their hands
I say – take this poetic fin, O Lord,
prophecy: a sun fluorescent: cloud vent:
front door: a pool party of overdue fins.
finds me as the landlord with spare key,

to maintain this coloured fin. God forbids
I'll remain a born-again image with cold eyes.
that I am not? An unlikely Adam's namely
with dark clay moulding bright destinies. So,
& use it for your glory / whatever gurgle
overflowing bathtub: runnel stairway: fist frail
Life abroad is a very lonely one but if grace
I'm another failed disgrace.

A little boy inventor soaked his sleeves
his diary. Wishing his slaving fears don't drown
tongue as gut-free sorcery. Never to let water
to always be prepared for the arrival of fishers
with a god in one's own image, free to make
& the remaining share of biblical bread crumbs.
really tell what you did with your life & money –

to keep afloat the paper boat he made of
his survival mastery, with the Igbo in his
scar you & if it does, cut a fin. It's a thing –
of men. To stay above the water & bond
a renaissance mistake of living on just nostrils
Until the day of reckoning when you can't
perhaps spent aiming at peeping reptiles.

There's nothing much my Jero self can do,
Aquatic workout with fins unmoved.
with faith in his sway of water & mud.
invisible majority Shakespearean audience
oily prayers / spillage, for it's a fin treated
a yesterday Naaman.
afford the minimum pavement required
winter patterning for a more grippy fin to survive

Just that one time.
You might fetch diegetic whistle of salt
collarbone to wash, treat skin irritations
behind my back to belch an American good

but to keep jumping from frying pan to water.
I thought I could just hold the priest's hand,
It's a tap-out fin; I slip as tightly held. The
at the shore hurl a sevenfold sheitan stones,
as a new being one instant, & the other,
I can't be long out here, I can no longer
for my continuance, let alone the pristine
the gossip pollution of this overdrafted land.

Now, I am not as gender fluid & saintly.
covenants from the hook-dug-well by my
or digest a borderline fishbone & still go
manner; colourlessly like an ideal water.

Border Manifesto

The earth isn't as spherical as oriented & it bothers me.
It is merely a catch-breath minute after another with
dramatic lots of belts return in evidence-like satchels.
That is, I might just be a sheet of paper, or a shit wiped
with passport diapers, or a piece of national cake,
or a mere Sabachthani – for Christ's sake.

Everything beeps,
everywhere clacks of pens,
of keyboards, of teeth & accents –
thighs are tearing; everyone is an incomplete
script's extra cast, traipsing into another as if
an improvised musical; in order of coincidental unison –
whole – disabled – leaping limps – wheels & wills.

Unlike me, many are little bodied worlds spinning
a spot in dizzy surrenders at the feet of rostrums, ready
for documentation of another cuss-titled bestselling
anthology of *Illegal* stories. Behind a fleeing man is a salt
woman, behind whom is a home burning down from
a kitchen fire: never to look back at the place they're
coming from. Where God, at a topmost hill, tolerates
the child's play of overcooking rock soup in attendance
to my daily bread prayers. So, the bubbles trickle down
to cause their world a third wife's kitchen mess.

I am here, a minute-long lasting power outage in my
brain circuit. For as those who had done this before
forewarned, I insist that my country is a distraction, &
I'm here to study. Pages flip, as if in quest for the correct
answer at the back of a maths textbook. Dog-eyed, staring
at my passport as if an image of an African museum
god brought right to his doorstep for a hand delivery.

It is the crazy need for continuity, as this, that certifies
why Christ could never be identified as a Black man.
Being my foremost therapy session with a white man,
I'm a round character of a developed short fiction:

just say it is a deflated soccer ball that spins past my yard to
his – is a boy just being handy. He could as well just take me in,
for a kickoff in his little court of numb thumbs & sticky red-
tapism. Or a tackle of papery fates. *Yes-sir* agama. Smile-carved
mortice dimple. Semi-seconds whistle. No mosquito stabbing
of corner kick pole to pore. A lickable finger. A branding, then
automated wormhole in which many-a-world brain drains.

Fourteen Days Silent Prayers

My father,
>   whose best art is silence. What have you to
>   say about these Omen I cook myself in despair to tell?

My belly mumbles indistinctly holding grudges against
>   your coin dearth; giving me fourteen days quit notice
>   in my own body. I equal a slim truth found underneath
>   the kitchen's remaining rice sack.

Today I wake again, hoping to find a forgotten
>   cash in one of my dirty pants. Noting an
>   underfed goat on the run from her owner for
>   days now, bleating outside, battling a scape with
>   its milkless teeth. I have nothing to offer, not
>   even the only avocado fruit spell our yard's
>   garden casts my Adam's apple.

Every sore living thing is frowned upon for
>   developing a cold; for being unable to puke a
>   morning egg without laborious cries unable to
>   work twenty-four seven: a messed-up pie formula.

Try not to be mad at me for sniffing or tasting
>   a little before offering you these words. Like you've
>   always taught that unholiness starts with eating before
>   attending Sunday services. Take this daily bread as I eat
>   out my lung in a quiet corner.

Hear a son ask his father not to be disgusted
        watching him throw himself into other men's
        mouths, to be torn open for a toast tradition.
        Living by a croissant bread alone in isolation,
        I expose my lung to a hopeful radiation,
        bleeding buttery thoughts, internally.

Don't trust I've been good. Simply ask.
        I spat to the ground and some pedestrians
        stepped on it. My throat lusts on soreness;
        confessing hoarse vowel as an art of breathing.

I have been meaning to ask:
        Would Omega bank the air we sip little by little
        for our unborn colourful kids, in the same
        forgery? That they might not cry out of existence
        as big breathless things whenever knelt upon in
        test for fitness, at an extra-plea-curricular karate hour.

Or, is it possible that the same trick of life everlasting fails
        the kinging king taking time off to sneeze into more
        stationary clay nostrils? 'Cos, Lord! This death
        of immortality contaminates.

My trying days are at the door, my dying days depend on
        your second draft. Patronize me, an unworthy earthling
        investment. I am pet free and my prayer garment is not
        so wool infested. My face is touch screen. Rub over and
        press your ground sturdy palm at my forehead's prayer button
        for a direct access to all that goes on in it. No need to
        invoke you till my spittle dries and my voice cracks.

Have you yet an idea of why true love is hoarded in Canadian
       seniors' palm grips, carefully strolling shelled crates of
       oxygen down the drives in rollator walkers?
       For your full-breath relationship lays off for not
       working – like that of our neighbour that becomes
       what the law pronounces for his wife who thinks he
       is becoming a threat to her; for he is everywhere she
       turns, even in closed eyes.

I, you – are pallbearers burying silence,
       respecting dying unmasked truths within
       the six feet distance between ourselves.

For I know you listen from the mast
       by the rainforest, I speak up and through my stuffing.
       That I may say the grace, not to be confused with
       "brace," "lace," "mace" or "craze."

I, your son, Owen, want to go out again to restage
       childhood with friends: play soccer, kick anything
       on the way – like a scared hedgehog wrapped in its spines.
       I promise not to get hurt in the defence position.

Asylum

in response to the Fulani herdsmen attacks in Nigeria

Far off, we follow the hearts of rivers in twists and turns like snakes through woods of grey mists and thorns. Of thousand silent squirms and treads, women bear tearful needles and threads and fragment pots, and sons and daughters to sow and weep and cook and eat and eat and die and we war for at least a bite. Besides, orphans like me wear their father's surviving khaki boots and cold eyes and dusty courage, through the greens and browns of days and nights. We have neither Simon to help us bear our crosses a little further in our skulls, across our shivers, to pierce our eyes with siren; nor Poseidon to gift us purebloods to drink, ride, live and leave; but far away from home, I hold a pile of my fatherland's sand in my left hand; although sieved, through my palm's fresh hollow, the hand I might never use to eat or catch flies or house silent prayers again. Planted in every soiled water I travelled, and look around and find a woman's neck, lost in lame pyrrhic dance movements in bead-less twirls of chopped waist and later, her son's bullet-holed legs, her daughter's crucified hands, feeble feet, the river behind us, and me. While the wind snatches our breath from our lungs and makes our skins burn, the kind of wind that makes us laugh out loud with each prick, I hear a cow moo from nowhere under the scorching moon, a dagger in my breast, a stain on my smile, a skip in the imaginary music, a pause to our meek steps, a red light. No home in this land too, only forlorn bones, in different forms; falling like drops of rain, in turns before the real dagger(s) trust our necks, hearts ... anywhere she deems safe, with her wealth.

Ad Lib

The afternoon winter wind's porous bruxism was unrehearsed
chant to my dying on a tart cigarette's butt same-smoke sip.
A flock of nanny blatted forward with unsymmetrical
horns to dig out, collect & mourn the remains of their
remains secreted in the corners of my mouth, the abyss
of my larynx. The grief dished their bellies like the
chords chewed when kneading my mother's kitchen
dough. In common, we've got eyes in widths of
suppressed tears, heroes-past vaporized into emerald
anthems sung to unroll tombs & summon away
chimneys' dark clouds produce. Now that I could tell
the cause of the uneventful *faces* I see in the flock
patterns of birds flying by the overhead power lines, I
mellow numerically, picking *faeces* deposits of stray pets
or fallen birds with my ashy hands. My girl, just back
from school – shadowy, curled-up in claws like a
painstaking kitty, joins me with a sac & oversize glove &
asks to teach her how to bury things with wings &
outdoor dreams:

"To name the fallen after a homeland, looking up & out
for overhead drones, escape planes or curses – while
digging, composing anthems in flagging synecdoche," I say.

Here or to Go?

The US
won't find the perfect aerial view
of an African woman's pot
as a nuclear hot spot,
neither could the UN meet suddenly
to cook curiosity about holed smokes
smouldering her pan's fried fish attacks.
They've learnt of her boys before:
state crabs with scissors' fingers to be
broken, easily, into their back pocket(s)
whilst assorted on false recipes.

After speaking to Màámi
over the phone,
I opened the homemade parboiled
militant stew she dished me
before travelling. Being unable
to lock my side-eyes off other passengers
nose conducts, I reptiled the Greyhound
bus's emergency exit – a tinted aperture
hoarding the strongest free Wi-Fi connection.

Screening global news – winded.
Allowing cookies while craving bagels.
Time multiplying speed, fixing briefer
distance, exempting my homeland's male
youths' wrists in fractured handcuffs.

A breather away
& at the pane prospect(s),
dreadful snake flattened the freeway,
starving road animals dodged the sunlight
from their rib cages,
flattened summer tires of couple travellers,
muted hisses of slied hitchhikers,
then road & internet traffic.

Stopover minutes
at the countryside's canteen,
some passengers' appetites were locked down
with finger foods of Japanese mushrooms look-alike
– assassin straw hats garnished.

Elderly men choked on belly jokes on the side:
"God forbid a reason for my spoilt housewife to cry
for external stir hands," flipping across a longer term
such that that time the following year's December,
a homeless person's fruitage remained a paltry snowman's
carrot nose. Should I have liked a goat meat,
I could've ordered the sort
of cud my parents had kissed severally
from the jaws of bellied men like them.

But "Not a sheriff's kneecap worn to my neck,"
remembering what the news reporter said,
slurping my foreign homemade spaghettini
in childlike eagerness to poke a catfish's belly,
when chanced to follow her mother
around market women's wares.
"Nom nom nom," they governed a raw rhyme taste
in my mouth like "Mom, mom, mom [...] see –"
a drone launched, from another angle,
in the form of insects buzzing about the meal
as if about bubbling intestines after soldiers' walkovers.

Squinting nostrils:
the spoon licked my lip's ring wound,
& my lips swore spicy air visits on dialects spread.
Then the bus hooted,
our owl necks readied.
(Un)fulfilled Newtons Sirs & Mas
began a stacked motion.

The clock had caught up on the clerk,
& the main meals were ready with excessive onion,
& lesser opinion about a passenger's favourite burnt flesh-part,
& a gender smile, "For here or to go?"

Fig. 1.2 Black Skin Diagram

tattoo treaties are the inks signed to my skin. fingers poised; pulping morning bursts to pores, burning from the driest of shafts. research-based; "loamy soil bears warrior genes thwacking a hydrant's nose bone. bleeding." shared loss, irrigating across my lid's boulevard. a quick Dolce fashion tryout – as quick as patting a plastic face into a police car's mirror & its back seat; delinquently air-wicked. free of charge. I lost my bearings yesterday. I had knocked doors to doors, my phalanges are peeling dry paints. I keep searching. a negro that once lost his son to the milky creek had his inflated body returned overnight. gerundial nonsense-perching by its bench today, a little boy chases after a balloon when he could've just waited for it to return. frostnip stiffness – not trying to grab a miracle by force, the wind paralyzes my fingers, my blood's not so warm. My prayers quiver for nothing, *"Something's supposed to rise from the sea. Isn't it?"* I wait a little longer as diehard believer would as if for a Black Friday; to get low-budget rosary & reel Sisyphus-like rocks with ease: a twelfth cassette – existential scene retake of the Black kid hoping on white geese for long, clean fingernails. "hwit" is the woman privileged enough to crate the sun in her shades while her child combat cake's sugary epidermis in its stroller. the remains grain its black apron with no stain to report for being nothing but a child. my patience whisk into the eventide & the water doesn't perform the same miracle – not twice in a week. had I known, I would've layered an icy faith over my animal skin & baggy jeans: a bare chest is no good branding [suppose for auctioning]. I have always had this sketchy illness of overhearing espionage walls chewing fat scandals into another's ears, "Henry ... is him?" "... her?" "... they?" "... them?" – that I'll look up to the sky of salt pinches on a burnt sacrifice & implore the Lord to save them from how they stare at a foreigner.

Terpsichore

If you're ugly, learn how to dance.
The song mustn't stop now, even if the
palm wine gourds get empty.

The green temple-dancers of the trees must thump
gracefully until the Nazarene orders them cut off. You
can dance if you can walk, you can sing if you can talk,
so walk and talk to the rhythm; fierce and steady, penny
flute; solemn and sweet, the chants; pleasant and choking.

Come on, boys, let's run the musical scale over and over, for
the old men and women, with library skulls and arid eyes,
swirling – leastwise countless seconds to smile and sweat
before the fume of the night come to hunt them like rats in
their holes and throttle them one by one.

Boys, though they call us drunk apes and some, daydreamers, we
will not submit our dreams to their jeers. Let's wiggle our tails along
our heads and feet in front of them and pluck their beautiful fruits
our grandfathers left unpicked ...
and if they don't want our tails to touch them, tell
them to back off the monkey festivity, far and
away. It's time to see the fate our steps have for us.
Peaceful rest on the breasts of a dozen angels.

Styling Pik

The first time I witnessed a man being pulled over,
I was on my way home from the barbershop.
I ran my comb through my hair as naive negro kids,
holding hands through their parents' master's plantation –
fading into outpaced ages by the panorama of clothing clouds.
Whether the parents should suffer for the obstinance
of their kids or not, something about them was always honourable,
worthy of a tailgate, capable of wielding blue lights –
it didn't have anything to do with age.
The world could wail for anyone, my friend, just so you may know –
one just needs to pick the wrong time to be in haste in life.
The man ought to know better about déjà vu semi-seconds
of an ugly chat, silly mistakes, panic click(s) or arrest attempt –
deadlier than cardiac: that is, to be pulled by the hair and
against the gecko asphalt concrete or chanced to lick blood
off his jaw, protesting curses disturbing the perch of a twin fly –
is the non-Shakespearean question of red and blue riot medication
radiating his tongue.
The scene laid on a stretcher attracted by him nasty with survival.
A portrait, taken and slid into any arm's pocket.
As if to be deliberately stored in red eyes, like mine, an onlooker
switching between pageantry stares and styles – an offshoot
of what's captured in the dark with a smartphone's camera, flash on –
the world coined into a cat's eye or a dog's – both of which could
be petty, but also adorable, clingier to beauty.
Weeks later, dandruff burned in my head
and my basic rules of firefighting changed.
A fleet of wind escaped the streets to hide in our curtains
and my skin bumped in a goose's wildness or ridges of veinless leaves.
It's because of my decaying brain, my mother said.

But it's a thing her man loved doing. In fact, that was how she met him
after he fled the courtroom's child-custody defeat and she hid him from shame,
and rumbled love down his throat like water down a clogged pipe.
So, if love, in a way, was above the law,
it was okay for me to romanticize blackness –
of arms and the men – of fists and the boys. With my head
daughtered in between her laps, her iron comb invoked incense from
my sizzling hair. No way any evil could dwell in our midst.
Mother reaped and displayed several lice before pressing them
against the ground. Then a thudding at the doorstep!
A thudding, of bulky rubber-banded free newspapers –
bagged as cadavers: as they've just returned something
or come for everything that belonged to us.
With the delivery man already thin into the street's curtain,
the comb I lost to the other day's sidewalk's
myth made the news – lifeless as roadkill but upright
at the front page's reporter's protesters' blur.

Fallen Walls, Mere Floating Portions

for Ejaz Choudry

Summer window fractures with an open-ended pestilence:
of kamikaze flies settling on black blood fresh from carbon cycle;

       of that life which matters – travelling back from offering itself
to the firmament – to relive a placard reason for (re)incarnation;

of Regis – a Toronto hybrid ladybird somersaulting her balcony; deck-neck;
causing a degauss effect – homely, like a toddler's innocence

when sharing a carelessly placed piece of magnet with its household's intolerant
LCD TV screen. Or diasporic, like the arrival of immigrants:
       ready to stay, as colour-works of upset streams.

My grandpa's neckbeard is ostrich-scarce. His bruise – red as a
       plagued pool, fresh from an out-bathroom fall,

is the foremost warning to the holders of his body.
       He dries up at every glance, his collarbones melt his breathing.

His orbs are goals of slow blindness. However, responsibility recycles. In
       the room of the living, I am coffee ready.

To add his whiteness jumble: "Salt or sugar?"
       He can't pick two words at a time, not even his favourite fruits –

lemon & Lebanon – from a browser tray.
       I school his daily Montessori –

"These are no pills. Repeat after me, they are not felons *on the run* in my throat,"
       before shutting down everything. Everywhere –

including the convenience store, he gambles in his head.

     91.1, correct decimal place of Canada's jazz FM, & no one's listening –

this is how humans suspect a god is using them without consent –

     witnessing armed spiders crawling a high-rise building
for gunpoint mental checks & balances; a piece of bloody music that catches

Grandpa's reflexes where its instrumental could see them.
     Clearly, apart from his refraining panic pulse.

Front page – *bulletin columns*: a flower vase shrills the street // because forensics can't
     tell the root // of the fire that deforested Horeb(ly) //

at Moses's eavesdropping sandals.
     Following page: ". . . as always, the world remains a snooker board with
Zuma masks emitting nuclear balls."

     Summer window welcomes ghoul appearances on a morning-star sunset
& of things pictorial under the orange safe light,

unread fine print Father's Day letter(s) litter my heart.
& you're not alone, kinetic dolls freak me out! But as Grandpa once said,

     "... until you start creasing into linens of goatee wrinkles, as
yards' Halloween emblem,

     into something so spooky but cool as hell."

Car Ride with My Father

We're in a giant car heading towards a brick
wall and everyone's arguing about where
they're going to sit. – David Suzuki

Just me and Dada this time,
adopting the street like a more preferred male child,
pursuing its tiny lanes to our nearest Sunday heavens
for service. The front seat is mine for my siblings have
found a god in their beds. I remember to put on the
seat belt, as well the meaning of some road signs, if not all.
Suddenly, he says a woman is like a vehicle.
But what do I know?

About getting one, her licence and registration.
The cost of accidental jokes, morning warm apologies,
driving according to limits, demerits or road tempers.
What about oil change, gaslights, growing marriage mileage,
nail-in-tires trauma, broken trusts and repair(s)?
About concentration, near-death survival or scrapping.
What technical know-how in the least?

Dada saves the world and blemishes his own, brown:
a merry-go-round case of used immaterial plastics and outdated
receipts. I never shut my eyes off things. "I am possessed by the
dark stuff cast off during prayers," he says at times.

For what do I not know –
about cleanliness and its godly fellow?
About an old thing's law of emotion, about the trap
in my silence? Repeating smiles into a writable disc
because family matters could be sitcoms sometimes.

I wind down the car window, forerunning the smell of
yesterday and the day before, beholding the side mirror
for the fates of pedestrian kids held by adults to cross
the roads, aiming for certain parenting volunteer hours.

A mad motorist damns a word or two at honkers.
Driving is simply a disturbed man's athlete. Or was he not
driven insane in the first place? Dada hits the brake suddenly,
I dangle loosely like the rosary and scenting pine trees
lacing the rear-view mirror's neck.

Stuck at a drive-thru's motor-thin corner,
they never have what I want; neither do I try to be in control.
Nodding to his intercom gobbled pronouncements. Coffee,
with a little bit of espresso like he hasn't expressed himself enough.
The road's freshly cooked granite sniffs us home sooner with
a thirsting for our woman's vapour vent forehead connecting
the face's fair tribal worry lines. Let's say, a relentless mechanic
in apron black-oiled with diagnostic hope. This is why I don't
take coffee; why I can't be trusted with a cupful of secret.
It makes me purge; I just can't retain it.

Flood

An adult doesn't cry, not like a kid at least.
That's why adults barely get napped.
Despite how far mine journeys, she returns home.
From work under a heavy rain, her face's droplets are
warm baths foreshadow. Though she'd lost her job prior,
but she's a basin capable of holding all drippings from
floorboards, even through to the living room. Her morning
prayers are nightly homecoming her aging self prophesizes.
With the right tiredness, her brooding grips firmly.
How long before she starts leaking depends on her skin's type &
tightness. As middle-aged, she can't wake the kids,
no matter how heavy she treads or slips & falls. She ages according
to conditions, beholden to one-too-many wound sites.

By storage room's entrance, she pauses & takes off her hat. She
becomes a trickling tank or hissing pop. The wall mirror bounces
       back   lightnings   in   quick reminders about why
she gets hairier every spring – bald lessons learnt from previous
seasons. Like, during winter, vehicle steering no longer belongs to
drivers. So, they need not beat themselves up whenever they drive
down wrong lanes.

Another winter without a vehicle could make an adult sob a little.
Or a divorce papered fleshless bedside; mostly common amongst
white folks as learnt, as if papers got nothing much to do with
people of colour if it doesn't bring in more papers.

Should the woman who runs off return for the rest of her stuff,
her children's worlds tilt & it's spring again. The home is tidier.
Wet shoes are leaned at the entrance properly. The Lord then
speaks through her, whose morning bad breath seeks flavour in
& favour from his mouth. It becomes her duty again to teach
the girl child of low-lying skirts areas, garden soil diggings & nail
painting. The fast-growing male child records adulthood as an era
of miscalculation & one too many injuries – often caused by
black ice at the front door entrance. Transparent like his mother,
until spring melt, when it gets watery like her love for his father
with no hypothetical reason for falling again.

Encore

i.   His left mouth's braced smirk toasts her a pinky gait
                    in karat fetter. Rosy songs coat her lips an Aramaic
                    sketch of a cigar's first click hisses. Dot silenced –
                    upon a cotton wedding dress. Every eye's entitled to
                    a peep in the hole. Hers, a perfect *do-not-perch* flies'
                    lash-skirt. Wingbeats are unwelcomed on this day.
                    Unless the flower girl's applauding costume could
                    feather a better melody. That the lady bleeds her heart
                    away, gazing at his diesel-fragrance brown padded
                    suit, her actual parents are missing like the "*cheese*"
                    to be bitten at photo minutes. Just that once, the
                    cleric advises fleshliness. That one generous sip
                    or oath bite of her thin fleshy mug. Bless the rented
                    musical instruments' recklessness to the choir's bop-
                    lift of her fabric in a long-drawn dawn-tint sudden
                    hymnal. That she orbs the spring season's horrific
                    half-eaten eye's apple, her lips are uneasy vermilion
                    climatic reaction to a layman-spelt cheilitis. Skin –
                                        a demise of undug layers. Wrists – half-broken twigs
                                        in an A-*men*'s hymen. For she hath walked into
                                        a helpless sanctuary in itself with a heart-written
                                        prayer in faith's forgery, a congregation of uninvited
                                        whispers BODMAS her salvation. Nearly leaking
                                        away her nostrils after his homecoming eye-meet.

ii.   The tower bell quits playing quick redemptive
draws, & birds scatter into their wings & upon
splashy still waters as our sons invade to catch &
pluck their feathers. Counting: one, two [...]
Like twice, had the cathedral's cast-off windows woo
our feet cheek by jowl, attending this screwy tapestry
strolls. The boys, still catching. The sun springing over
her parents' dead bodies. She, streaking away at the
palette hour. Venting grudges against her makeup
artist till a never-coming embarrassed kingdom.
Catch! A big ditch in his pocket; only begotten bile
stuck on a visioned bachelorette's strip pole slightly
akin to the pulpit's "INRI" first aid red cross branding.
Her misty breathing filters into picky whimpers.
Pluck! Tugging her gown as if filth, "That you may paint
me a deliberate mistake," heaving a chilly sequel.
"Don't turn, don't quiver, don't look back at him."
Because everything's at stake – her kitchen steak,
cooked beauty, unlidded pride. "He will do his pretty
stingy chase, but just leap & fade. Glide & fade."
She squashes an unfallen roadside tree-fruit &
hustles the streets till she tickets a winning fog.

Rap Sheet

(*i*) My mama's obsessed with uniforms. She wished I grew quicker to end up in one. It's ours to birth our likeness naked and to fold its slanderous skin into an unbranded up and down. "Wow

wow wow." I pulled up to her in a soft hand-on-waist pose and she's hooked. All I wanted to become was a rapper. A poet, she bartered. Not in my right senses could I let a spelling bee sting me

to starvation of rejected manuscripts. Facts and nothing but fax. (*ii*) It's winter and I'm shedding a new skin; a confused yellow with a little touch of brown. My blackness is turning a muddy poetry.

There's a mix-up somewhere in my dermis. I'm maturing, sticking to things I don't know, not this elementary nature's art: sketchy reptile in hoody and silent prayers. Just "wow wow wow," I ain't seen

none like this before. I am eating up in malnourished rusts. How many more percent of oxygen could I hold? Or trees may I unhang or burn to ventilate my lung longer? Mama knew better but she bit the

kitchen's rug's dust before she could whiten her teeth on a June date. I'm left to maintain this uniformity myself. (*iii*) So, loamy-boy, uh? Oh no. That's my stage name. James, look – as stated in

my CV. I've got no more bars except they'd like to put me in one. My cufflinks pin me tighter to this shaggy "T" that I may seem to them one of the good ones. Even without headlock records nor Rasta

hairlocks, unfortunately! Then a longer gaze through the office window to the public bus like a deportation plane's intense view of clouds putting up Juneteenth cotton-picking show, before

untacking my cufflinks and rubbing my face to reality, like taking a systemic fate into my hand as a bleaching lotion. Like Bruh! No other way but to make a living on time or do time.

Who Hides a Chased Thief

hath a Jericho heart and belly that
fall prey to flies musical band encircling
her ears. After choiring a whirlpool
pose, she wads pearl liquid away the
wall's casement, whistling woe at its
only limping metal wing. Saturday night –
and disco lights war are still very much on.
Any man missing in bed is known to be
lost to a profane rapture. He, with triplets
caught in a cast of sleep's net, wheezing
mosquito coils, is on a night shift watching
for that not lost in beaded chambers.
She, who chooses to scream into the
night, does so, muting her wakeful
wee kids in holed vestments.   *Where?*
Another, capable of locking down a breath,
drags home hers by his torque and belt, less
a propane cylinder weight – with her kid
sticking her life-death thoracic.   *This side, that side –*
the night somehow crawls out of its hue
in burglary toes into a homely movement.

*Of the previous night's robbery, she let
the hefty man in, herself, says the neighbour.*

Him, still dawning on glinting gapes, regular
as clockwork: bald, deaf, western goon in petrol
blue frock, smart and tuck, breakfast on dry
household grocery from an On the Run convenience
store – and hopes on the chaste of either of them to
pick the first sentence and slam as a bass curse or
simply watch the rumour travel by his earholes, blindly.

Not Every Father Leaves

My negroes ache in blues' rhyme schemes & second-hand
instruments by whining them scrappy throats in alien tunes of sonnets,
stuck at them vocal cords' borderlines. The tunes crash their scarce nights in
form of returning revolutionary stack of fathers brung away – spat from
holes of short-term rented brasses; non-smoke-free ductworks!

Blues hisself witness these run-throughs –
of returning Pops bipedalling them reformed asses from bass to arm,
reaching for the city bulbs outside them irons. But false alarm –
their anklets beep. 'Cos what Blues' Mama once said, "No pops ever loved blues."

So, dead be the men resurrecting with little clues
of (legitimate) survival. Till cracks do them apart at a felon farm,
quite soon a harvest of tuber as fate in the shape of a firearm.
Shoo! Shoo!! No refund sweat for them tapping shoes.

"ABBA! ABBA!!"

To keep the rest an urchin sestet in my jar throat, leaving them
mountain melodies out of my mouth – by the bloodstream's canoe,
raising my ape skull above the water, I salute my sight on them
pregnant landscapes ahead.

Blues set hisself on fire during them demonstrative musicals.
Breathtaking. But my organs fail to uphold a live tune. Ask, as he shall,
about my ~~unkempt~~ receipt upon return, my eyes' sea levels paroled
downpours upon my unshaven, metropolis lids.

Down South, homegrown *Mimosa pudica* still stretch them palms of
semen sighed from many teenager-years ago.

"You done already seen me, Jamal?" I ask.

"Here! Here?" Blues singalong.

Of these short days acquired in a decimal refund we may never get, this is the purple prose you seek:

"Your mama hadn't been lying her black lips from can't say to can't say. Love just ain't enough. Mothers leave too."

Pear Trees Hanging Minor Negroes in Tie

Case study of Emmett Till

(*i*)   Parenthesis: parental advice, or sectioned debate about a
teenager's biological similes – Like his mother,

he is Lombroso's spoon count of delinquency in an ugly skull.
Like his father, he's an Afro series' (un)auditioned felon cast member.

A boy's imitation flaw is stuttering –
"Yo! Mama" in his first poem, scaffolded on a journey.

Like his friends – homophily; home training locked on new Versace hairdo,
wanted face(s) in dreads embroidery headshots.
It's always the pear tree putting pressure on the other garden trees.

(*ii*)   Sterile mornings are dreams deducing themselves.
          A morning could only be golden as a baby's cereal.

          [Too many awkward phrasings]

          From backstage is the deafening Jim Crow's SFX, also a
          cricket's hallucination of sex hustle / victim hit-on as if with a
          Punjabi batter abreast her tournament screams.

(iii)   "*Em, I, Double-S, I, Double-S, I, Double-P, I.*" Vowels accursed to a brief statement when asked where the safety button is on a girl's body, when in danger.

"*Em, I, Double-S, I, Double-S, I, Double-P, I*" becoming the shortest river in the gang of broad migrating wings & steel throats.

Until guilty, innocence is an alternative sin – even when not an American daughter but blames should've remained on the game controller(s), home & away.

Vows accursed – if one could tell a midnight son to prevent whistling at the day, & take time to adjust his knot's tightness, consider the gauze of his protest's blisters.

May he choose to run from kissing a slanderous knife & his godly mother would not have to prepare a strangled meat towards his fifteenth birthday.

Home-Away

1. Crowding the university's viewing centre while academic finals are still on: with own goals, blankets, lecture handouts – no one can curse or pray for Nigeria like we do. Our study alarms are clueless cues for tomorrow's blank space on exam question papers. We hope the prof doesn't show up as a demonic referee. I, specifically, hope he sees through as a nice immigration officer for I'm done taking his sociology class one more time.

2. It's understandable that we might be losing through the first half, considering how long it takes me to figure why I prefer the team on the right to score the left regardless. Last time it took me half an hour to define the migration terminology for a country betting a handicap on its players away on a foreign soccer defence project. So, I'm twice shy to memorize & be able to tell of the course documentary about a paper boat, the size of a cap, as a child's play by the waterside. Who is his mother, a rude guy asks. The joke couldn't dry the sweat rivering down my palm – channelled dams.

3. Then – "Nile won. Won!" On the camera's blur, returning waves are jubilation somersaults. The oafish formation of fishers & whispers paid off as barefooted celestial mortals in half-crescent casting call, outlining the penalty sandbox. His mother must be proud & his country must be mad for not taking the advice of the Egyptian commentator on saving his pharaonic scalp from water suicide by getting a neme & sunglass to witness this day. In defence of wildness, armpit & fart odours of the house's future leaders, is the instance of the teardrop of a little girl documented as fish's raw skin rip on an over-fried pan. A close-ended prediction with neck nods as if twisted twice with labiodental strangles under sacks.

4. But "Nile won. Won!" the rescue team's scripted response – just who the hell is this beach who ought to be sweeping the streets of Lagos? He should even be sold for nothing! Only those outside the field see the game clearer & could tell these embarrassing things. What the night turns them into: da-dum breathers sick with cold burnt chests & many more other climatic conditions like refugee returnees – defeated by paperless governing bodies of water.

5.   For it's the duty of water to return all, in disarray of skin & newly sewed ugly uniform. One-leg injured players – kite forth as darker flags frowning on a second leg with eight-feet-wide monkey goalpost. Amid mouth-watered flowery honours, they stand steadfast like Seme Border's *Aladura* candlelights to the shore's wind, peeling like banana waxes in prayerful hands. We don't mind tearing up our slips like a textbook page for malpractice but the temper of tomorrow's examiner or policemen that bet straight win of stray bullet in our chests.

Aladura: White garment church member.

Migraine Thesis

C.W.: drugs, war / violence

(*i*)   At Miami depot escaping a despot, bright children fold American dreams
to their blinds

       & later set free their sights to seek different lights.
It looks simply – like a bee, sea – whatnot.

       Adults scold as usual. Waters are tongues' masterminds, castling
the younglings' shelters to liquid alights.

(*ii*)   I cry,
"O America! Only thee God hath trust in, to recruit refugees

To invade their homelands with vindictive delight."
Some parents fold up their kids' affairs in Soviet lees.

Others, mouth-gashed, as if vulnerable to a fountain faucet's fright.

(***iii***)   *"O America! Draft me in the first-three rebellion commandments."*
Bay – relenting ship-vows & modern homecoming desperados,
of silly strategies & resolute troops as
Pigs – snorting dirty drugs in camouflages.

(*iv*)   Say I lack citation because home is not a reliable source.
These words are not mine –
mine are bomb-clatters deposited in passersby's faces, *"Bomboclaats!"*
I don't mean to scare the children / alter their dreams' form.

Tell me, what country's anthem does not have "O"
segregating ad libs?

A crazy demo on the fade,
       "Sip me a Kennedy weed & see how high
I could pilot a B-26 beyond a Cuban sky."

Landed or a Cue to Go Back to Your Country

I found my papers in a foreign girl's diary at a dirt cheap
home-away exchange rate; any shit per sheet. Hearsay

about love for men of my kind looks to be right. Bare
primary-colour yoke whisk of sun cracks into

fire-fry pan rounds. Even so her needle-neck kiss experiment,
black face skin care routine & non-existent dance steps,

are getting weirder – she's my gap tooth's fur trustee blowing
phonic foghorn & digging into my pores for safety. The first

flakes of snow hail in heavy seraphic pebble protest & I am
curtain layered & translucent, keeping an eye on the Chinese she

ordered. I've never met who could chomp an entire ethnicity so
satisfactorily. Having had an early sour taste of the Negroni she

unlidded since yesterday, I still can't tell of its magic on my cough.
The call with my mother is a visual niggle of my neck looking

thinner than her hope in our homeland & if I am to remember well:
that despite my straying, I am still my father's bullet. I should return

home sooner for her friend's beautiful & well-trained daughter. But
come to think of it, no one wants to return home empty-handed.

Emily just wouldn't let go of me being too tired to feed her cat today.
The name panegyric I gave her in my language rings shaky diacritics.

The season's surviving anopheles try to make a helipad of my skin /
a final emergency landing on a landed individual's yard. "Takbir! Allahu

Akbar," chanted our newcomer neighbour. "Shut the f*ck up,"
a pair of Saul shoes munches the entrance in an exact cringe at gum

chorus of a toddler's denticles on Doritos. Tsk! These people.
They never get used to it nor us.

Herbs & Psychosis

I had a night in which everything was revealed to me. – Sarah Kane

I speak of it again –   knowing I shouldn't when an adult speaks.

Head down, listening.   Fixed stares at the sunset lagging behind. The human body

is an archaic language   not everyone understands. I shrimp like an aged

African storyteller,   self-handcuffed to spine. Just like my father's grandfather –

an uncaged captive   with all old-age charges dropped against him,

yet tied to an illness   or the other. *"There's a curative leaf for that,"*

he'd say rest assured   in his sickbed. That is why our people don't die young.

They live to see   what will become of their procreations. Ready for work,

ready for school –   my stay-at-home order remains; to stick to my medications.

I am awake earlier   than usual, curious about a nightmare about a pipe

my windpipe   breaking. Plumbers charge too much for repairs.

Too much water will be lost   & the hydro bill will become double.

Nothing worries me   more than the pills that will be found therein, stuck.

My husband   & children will despise me for that. Between those who sleep with a bible or

before grabbing

wrong with me.

chewing stick.

If in need of healing,

Memorable, like

but listen to

weighing down

Head down, with

locust beans –

broken climate

phone under their pillow, one awaits a call. Like a revelation,

a scripture to pray. However, there's a leaf for what's

A stick of weed, I think. My forebear would prefer a

He'd advise against any sort of needle on my skin, too.

he'd beat about the bush with cutlass adages. Basic.

Queen premier's incantations. He'd advise not to interrupt

all he has to say. So, I am standing – feeble, my head

my tiny neck like a mushroom. A little poke can flake me out.

fixed stares at footprints or his mouth as he chews raw

"To wash my mouth with gin tea & breathe in my backyard's

& simply live like everyone else in the family."

Orthoepy

Why should I have chosen

between my mouth mud-up in a combo of brown oral,
scarlet cured eyes, salty coughs, powdered nostrils,

rotten teeth's raw menthol resin, trembling lips like mumbling zips

for bearing a *pubic* conduit unwelcome riders travel through
its stop signs, roughly, towards a pretentious sorry traffic?

– because doing what needed to be done

includes matching the street's silence – bulging my dodge:
a patrol without a radar nor installed red-light camera(s).

No one will believe whether it was a green light or not.

"So, what do you say?"
– that the first time could be the devil's work after a libido deluge

– that this day, I must place my chest down for a mammogram

as if against a carbon paper's first draft: without fear of *radiation exposure*
to something other than my kitchen's microwave.

– or a hardihood, that charges one guilty for swelling in puberty

with an upturned sentence, meeting with an apostle's crucifixion fate.
You ask, "What witness has this little thing lived to bear, Jehovah?"

but Peter does not find me worthy of his trust. I am tender with his pace

like the first time wheeling a bicycle, reciting anything to remain focused.
Still, I am running into you, into the bush, into the poles. Trying again

and again, and again – even though he asks why I didn't say something
after their zips mumbled to my trembling lips.

Wait a Sec

after Claudia Rankine

You're asked to wait for a few minutes to be called into the office earmarked to you at the immigration centre. You scramble on documentation updates; no time to delay. The officer who attended to you talks on the side over the phone – covering her mouth as if telling a white-collar secret to its mouthpiece. Your eyelids bulge from not sleeping after your night shift before resuming in the morning. You're heated up in hastiness of people's reasons for wanting to stay.

Their child. Their life. Tomorrow.

Your head is getting as light as the pain reliever container, joggled-empty. No two pills per-the-day. You're approximately one twenty-six minute-hand dizzy to your therapy appointment, you bring out a pocket mirror and contour brush from your handbag in maintenance of your face's coffee-coloured foundation. Then two women, fair and fresh from the city's honks and vehicles' emissions, walk past you and into the office. The officer's migrating fingers tap her keyboard into your awareness, so you leave your seat to ask what's up. Whether she remembered to write your name down or if it was spelled correctly. No time for delay. She asks if you do not see her attending to someone: heavier and louder than a gravel slam. Then you feel your heart's pulse in your head suddenly. Your neck stretches in "N-word" reflex. Not that you like appearing autistic, but you're grown to know that there're more severe consequences for looking away.

As if you aren't someone too!

Returning to your seat to exercise more patience, the women exit the office for the entrance of a couple more: uncalled. A time-lapse dizzy viewpoint like the city centre on weekends. As diagnosed by a physician, you have Cotard's delusion. Tallying your religious leader's vision about you having the walking corpse spiritual problem. Gentlemen do not see you whenever they are ready to settle down. How about gentlewomen?

Within a sec, the cops arrive and one of them whispers with the lady who attended to you, sharing spitty vocables, looking in your direction. He sees you. Only a white man in uniform could, anyways. He shadows you in space and style and asks you not to resist the catchy irons he quotes your wrists like an unsuitable suitor. For you don't look like the lady in the card you tendered, your words will grow feet against you – should you choose the moment to practise pronunciation(s).

It turns out to be a regretful apprehension. You tell your therapist suing them might not be good for your record. You are turning green around the gills and your stretch marks are tearing more widely. Your stress-burnt cheeks map northern sunburns; you clearly don't look like yourself in your pocket mirror. Yet, you want to stay because your travel card is still green. You can work. You are ready to – anytime.

Even though as the living ghost you are, just within-a-sec, you are another black file earthed in the police's cabinet(s).

Alibi

for Akinfolarin Pojo

SITUATION:

A few farmers align with sack clothing and dry leaves in hair. One wears a nose mask, vinyl gloves, stethoscope, while another holds a scalpel, suture and a needle. One bears a sickle while the others play a solemn rhythm with a gong and pair of bongo drums. The farmers are also the Thespians.

FARMER 2

Doctors being better than farmers is an outdated debate. Tap the back of the hand like a newborn's unresponsive chest. Its heart withdrawing from the percussion band.

FARMER 3

A sneaky, lazy live-band member costing the audience a minute more sort of silence that follows a ward's self-echo like a dusty unoccupied event hall.

FARMER 1

(Claps twice.)

Ta-ta! Calling upon a stone cold response. Oh, what is life without an infant being generous with tuneful tears; life-large downbeat 2/4 time signature renditions.

FARMER 3

I, a more experienced stoner, give my all to fall for this fourth-generation second-hand temptation.

FARMER 1

Palms beating the drum are swelling. The skin beaten is hurt. Oh, bread turning to stone!

FARMER 2

The thin from its belly is the thing about its neck. Oh, stone turning to bread!

FARMER 3

Tiny Tears! Tiny Tears!! Tiny –

FARMER 2

We shall worry about asking for forgiveness later, but now we will take whatever yeast breath, broken shock absorber, keys to the city and every other tempting chance bestowed upon us in applause.

(FARMERS, *shuffle*.)

THESPIAN 2

Time flew so fast that we couldn't catch the sight of its wings. We're not surprised – for actors are witches that fly from end to end of the stage's wings. Though, I've fallen into the orchestra pit once.

THESPIAN 3

Such awe. Ashes of our tradition set alight is proof of baptism. We, the remains of the powdery yesterday the firefighters tried but failed to extinguish. We, the cause of today's fire and tomorrow's drill – starting from the slightest meet of our sweat and fierce eyeballs with your worry hearts. We wake up with a deadly odour from our mouth because of the decay of the words, we left unsaid from years ago.

THESPIAN 1

Yungba-Yungba* was our last dance contest together.

THESPIAN 2

It all started with pretence. So, pretend to listen as if to the Caesarean theatre's quelching decorum. We are wanderers from a Phoenix of Arizona; displaced from home with our skin peeling in evident layers. A reason we are two-four-six-faced creatures.

THESPIAN 1

You can say, just a little rain and then, earthworms' invasion.

THESPIAN 3

That rain that strips at our presence can't flood us. Not anymore.

THESPIAN 2

Beware of forgetting that we are pretenders. Amoebic, lining up in false feet as stand-ins before the main actors come onstage. So, while you can, cut yourself on quick, sharp stage scenes, or watch how you get gut cut-open by role-played surgeons with sharp dictions, sentences that could sew your bleedings.

THESPIAN 1

Big Tears! Fat Tears!! Big Fat –

THESPIAN 3

Don't axe me no question. Don't axe us anything. We are the emergency exits for your souls, your cyclic dream's ritual dancers. Fallen angels landing on their feet. A crowd of one-half boys claiming to be men.

THESPIAN 1

We don't have much advice as we've just got our wisdom tooth removed. But you should know that we're the masquerades behind the curtains, flitting this lit stage together, witch-nosed, "Ta-ta, tattering!" on bundled twigs.

THESPIAN 2

Thus, as we exit ourselves, pretend you're our alibi.

(THESPIANS, *shuffle*.)

FARMERS (*In unison.*)

Yungba-Yungba was our last dance contest together and this is as much as we could harvest this season. Reap Pojo! Reap Pojo!! Reap Pojo!!!

Blackout.
Then theatre full light.
Curtain call.
End.

*Yungba-Yungba and the Dance Contest is a stage play by Femi Osofisan

Window-Shopping

If we know our place, our men are side mirrors.
As you see, from the other side, where they don't
really think anyone else matters, as we do, our
women are starched in slurs of their supremely fused
sand, soda & lime men – a mirror solution,
that makes a dummy formula of our women
in a glass view of stagnant things all dressed up
to promote a Black Friday's *napkins-on-sale*.

Ages have passed now,
& the glasses are shattering into grains like corns
filling the palms of the homeless man at the bus
stop feeding pigeons illegally. They know how to
pick men like that up & return them as if
recycling fibres, or weaving ready-made in a knitting
pin's art mastering of picking on desperate yarns
into customized forms of:

i. *mammy* – breeding sons to run *Grand Theft Auto*,
ii. *matriarch* – androgynous, with their men's bones to teeth, &
iii. *welfare mom* – of a dozen downfallen mammary glands,
plus puppies' support claims.

So, the more jobless I get, I roam about malls to buy
some time I can't afford in the first place. No
mannequin outgrows its show glass – & not that it
really matters like the firmament roaming the sea by
its racial Kármán lines. Science just got too many lies
to feed. I pick one – that unfed genes hinder height
growth such that I now know the stagnant ground
for our women's upward mobility.

I don't have to – these comparisons draw themselves –
on a *one-by-a million-inch* joist of nailed martyrs. Of a
brown woman so gorgeous that she moulders in
crumbs. Of their men envisioning an invasion of
figurines in whatever market. Of something weak, nasty
like dandruff or deadly like sickle cell. Of high heels not
tall enough to help reach a cupboard's top. I just don't
buy that this is what being free from cliché should be all
about. Because, how any different would they see the
women of their yards?

Yankee Boys

So, a man had strayed to the Queen's room more than once?

[...] well, it's not much of my business, but I know that a Black child
is a ticket or etiquette – an exile ground for passage.

His mother's scarves are nylon maps for her man's whistle freights –
manning up as voice breaks in throats, tighter than spectral seats

left in buses deserting north, & with heads fell off their dump
trucks' bumps, they grow sandy as arid whispers gathering

in a vow to keep the fresh corpse as secrets.

[...] often in films, upon a partridge flown far away
to nestle a diaspora climate, is the paper-thin tendency to heed

a fraud wind knocking on the door for directions.
Then he perambulates a *Queens Street*.

His curious teeth fork as a careful comb brushing western shock over
Yeoman Warders' unkempt cylinder Afros. Guns-up in attention,

"To the sky we swear to shoot you wandering blackbird!"

[...] so, another blackbird I know is jumped in the wind with his
wings' stolen / broken. He survived a living pharmacy

with pathetic hygiene: weighty poop in sagging pants,
shirt stinking with streets' sweat. The last born of his family learns

to identify what a black sheep looks & smells like.

[...] the day breaks into another's house through locked
windows with the dinning table's *Pepsi* manners gassing his

low-key *Coke*. Like the wind hath lost its way, yet again.
The ground's dependency turns the bird sprawling with

an abdominal reason for passage. Everyone then plays along
when a cold joke is told – freeze! The safer way of keeping

another from falling / vowing to keep another secret.

Evening Bird

Dedicated to Pius Adesanmi & the lives lost on flight PS752

Dearly to the sun, your serpentine fins embraced bluffs,
tripped the morosely linking earth
& the heavens with howling wings.

// a poet; a feather //

You became lines of sun-split stanzas,
warping seas underneath you.
You hooted ecstatic stunts, *"everyone deserved a sunbath."*

// a feather; a dreamer //

You didn't have enough sleep, you ne'er dreamt.
You imitated a night-disciple, zombied your hands over your
shoulders & blurred God in the face.

// a dreamer; a tossed coin //

Unbelievers chose the head, the tail, & I chose none. But
you burned blue through your gasps in awe & palpitated as
volatile balloons from the nose bone of a knitting needle.
You gasped fireworks & heaven echoed fossil fuels.

// a tossed coin; a fallen-pious angel //

Against the hard clicks of a gong & strikes of
human-skinned drums, the spotlight's moved to us in thick
tears & our tight gullets, a tourniquet. We're displaced –
cruised police gossamers with our feet sweeping metallic
feathers. Our hands with a kettle douche in a pool of grief,
one flopping a portrait & the other a lantern. The debris
clasped our locust jeans to melting plastics & iron shafts.

Evening bird, as you watched tears leak from our hard
eye gazes & haven't yet discovered enough proof or
theory on risk society, please you may
Fall! Fall again & alone!!
like a thunderbolt, but far away from our smiles.

If Only

love could be   that front slab   of gossip[s] dissolving on your tongue,

         or the large weevilled wrapper
     rolling around your falling fruits & waist

before you leave your children no lesson notes
     to report to daily dooms that remind you that you're a river,
         & you meet with dusk's sunlight; that had warned you
         already of burning your skin & your feet.

Is it love you spittle of your son's face when he wakes to watch the news of
how the cattle you rear goes beyond your armpit to drink souls in moos?

     He curses you for being too careless for revealing your bum as twerks,
     at the village square, to a piece of unheard destructive-music

& promises never to bring such a lady home, to you, as his wife.
If only you swear too by the iron, cross & moon & dust your shoes,

     wash your white thoroughly, polish your black, scamper
     your synthetic grey hair for dandruff[s]

& learn better ways of squirming & polluting any garment with an open sore, faith
would be woven into your skullcap as you unfurl each morn, noon, twilight.

It's faith whose hand holds back your hair while you're sick of oozing
bloody sweats,
     burying your children with your hands, in your scars.
     Tomorrow you love any man ready

to toss his tongue, & enticing wares into your valley

beyond your collarbone, & sell in advance payments,

& never give you your change.

No one will teach you how to carve love on your babies

like wooden figurines, with your   breath weaving their throats.

No one will tell you –

a healthy temple is justice's asylum. Last days will call you

doubly while you've got one hand on your note, & you'll

consider balance before payment.

Driving Test

after McKinney

(**1**) You grant your driver examiner the licence to instruct you in phonic Ebonics because no one ever understands anything you say. Follow the path that doesn't crave a black blood, she says during your third driving test at a Greater Toronto Area. So, you clutch diagonal away from herbs, sapwoods & the roadkill of puma-doomed creatures. (**2**) As a trauma-informed driver, you watch out for school kids crossing countries in sloppy feet. Your extracurricular race with family had never been past unwelcome dreams beyond the clouds. (**3**) On your next turn, you are looking over your shoulders in fear repeatedly, like experienced passersby at Jane & Finch's intersection. Constructions never cease; the roads are too wounded. (**4**) Decamp into ramps of small intestine twists, she says. But driving alone, you've always avoided highways – for the fear of breeze shaving crazily at your vehicle's chemo head, other drivers bullying your sluggishness or the spotlessness of speed guns with kilometre bullets aiming at your windscreen's chest. But boys in your age don't mind masturbating the wind, she adds. (**5**) On your first test, after noticing Simcoe's lofty land mass in a hazy lettered landscape, you nodded into Barrie. Your car engines grew nervous, sick & then jerked into a historical recall of some Mexicans dodging traffics to disembark Wasaga Beach on an over-speeding wave. That's why you don't choose to do your tests at other nameless distant cities. They pass almost everyone who could steer a bit of an anger in their ankle but you. (**6**) As you return, the cloud is wrinkling, & the evening is becoming a burden to the examiner's sight but yours remain catchy for every vehicle's print that pleads every mind that reads. (**7**) Streetlights are dashing lustre against the Lord's prayer your summer tires cast upon the road's sharp yellow margins. Your heart is failure pious. Park here for now, she says, until the court calls for another hearing the government will carter for some of your needs. (**8**) Wut? She means to park parallel to wherever peace seems to reign despite friendly obstacles ahead / behind. You collect back the licence to be sure you've been hearing the right thing all along. No, things have been going downhill. When she asks you to perform three-point turn, you don't want to go back home, you say. "What do you mean death awaits you at the port?" The language-textured Plexiglas in between wipes hazy odour barrier. (**9**) [red light camera ahead] She hits the brakes for you on her end. "That's enough! You should go back home," she tells.

I Know

If you ask me, I may know why the caged bird cries.

I used to think of deserted water as the loneliest,
then I realized the sun's the creepiest. It peeps from
the sea's blanket with its hands within, looks
around and reptiles far away into the sky, quickly.

The earth is now spiral, like a snake chasing its tail.
I know because time is the only thing moving.

"I" is a candle with an invisible wick, burning dots upon itself.

Walls do not send fire upon a matchstick scrubbing
its forehead against their bricks, because I think I
smell the kerosene of
"the third world war" like "Christ is coming soon."

I'm hypnotized; my beak does not fit in the cage's iron. There
are voices hidden in these walls;
I hear cries and giggles that are not my own.

Something, someone, somebody farts in the air –
we, us, our soldiers are fighting unsure wars.

The clink-clank milk squeezing out brown, black tea is
an outbreak hitting my head, skull split, rebellious
soldiers?

I know I have sinned. I know isolation is
idolatry – worshipping the deity of separateness
and loneliness. I know because the wind is the
only thing outdoor to stir the children's swing.

Steadfast

Every time we shoot for the stars,
we should also remain behind to witness the sky
mourn the loss of its dearest glitter,
for the prophetic gunpowders
we let up there ain't enough to makeup.

Alif

Habibti,
What mountain should I scale?
She knew I saw her
come take away your bags of weed
no gardeners' children no more.
saying, *I dreamt* about burning within
look in her direction: a gist punishable by grudge.
when she looks at me, she says I slip her memory
I'm unsure if she prophesizes that my room
homeless. Oh my! My premolar tooth detaches
while all I must do is to pick a pet's name:
Habibti, I think
battle with a layman infantry retreating –
of her womanhood. Red sends her the screams
Still she insists seeing me, what do I do?
that there's no difference between our prayers.
shape of an idol's breasts?
Arabic, she says, mirrors true alphabets.
left–right; into my zest, her eyebrows browse
Then, I am surer it isn't me she sees.
is this mountain safe for me to scale?
to mumble, sing with my ears trimmed in

I have seen a girl naked.
What Psalm verse should I flip into?
& I don't know how to say to my guys,
from my room. I don't wanna be friends with
If they ask *why?* I would be unable to lie,
a river during self-baptism. They will for sure
Habibti –
but she sees me; as sizzling wax's slim hope.
will burn soon & leave over a thousand apes
from her jaw's similar guerilla army teeth
I just can't pronounce this vocab in mind.
it's not me she sees. It's like 3-D hologram
in bloody feet; fleeing into the street lit city
way, so she wears black.
She says: *I-slam, she slams*, then *we slam* –
How so if my bed's furniture is carved in the
She washes her sins over God's feet on Jumats.
When I feel her bosoms' seeds germinate
deeply into her narrow gorgeous nose bone.
But, Habibti,
Is this the sweetest of all Psalms
between her teeth; alive & simple like, Alif?

Not My Underpants

but law remains everywhere – doesn't it? in the
cooking bowl – dingy fry pan, the stodgy attic – the
weekend stinks of used-cloths' baskets – wet shoes
pinned to the entrance's wall – for dehydrating arrests,
door grips' electron.

in (un)assented salt containers in the kitchen cabinet.
plenty of soup cookers, few reliable pots. the way you
sit with your limbs emptied or folded – in harvesting
unripe berries on minors' panties – dry humps & sore
notes, straightforward sentence – adverbial phrase –
to *rot* & *rot*.

public eyes, loitering passersby, handicap parking spots,
in the black women's weekly support groups meeting – the
hoody slide-in-palms of pharmacy nylons – in Indigenous
despair & tepee repair – vigil eyes & ceiling fans tootling
fevers; shadows replaying darkness.

in loving a weird neighbour as yourself, in form of
abrading palms & global warmings – in
memorizing Roman figures & taking *paterfamilias*'s
shits.

every time, I've made an ark of my tongue & a covenant fed to a
native accent – avoiding the English dungs my forefathers
somewhat stepped into, I insist this land is mine
& my body is the land. Like the last time,
I'll tell death not to touch my hair or the raven flying off my lingerie.
or else, we're gonna have an omnipresent problem.
a lawsuit to begin with.

Identity Syntax

A child has more than a language baptism
after its olive wobble sentences and spit bubbles.

My mother's tongue is the same subway to Pennsylvania.
Bad English was a suitcase she came with to the diaspora.

Should a US missile go missing, it would be a floss in between
her canines. Her peninsula is belted to the root of her family tree.

Pearls of wisdom are traditional black rubbers melting her
hairstyle. Most times, I get nauseous from the hastes of migrating

train lights and whirlpool turn to the directions of exile compasses.
When the whiteness of everything turns a monarchy glove claiming

my teardrops, my mother quits her appointment with her dentist to
help respell, "N*gga is a honey wrap every human wants to tongue."

Coffee Shop

For now, Father, in his birthday suit // requires no necropsy // but a cup of coffee [don't ask why]. He disappeared two days ago // without taking his prayer mat and beads along with him // then, I confirmed his days are numbered // like Mother's, // who spat on his face one day and drove off // and felt countdown hunch over her steering wheel like an old woman // knocked against a coffee tree // in the middle // and yet, never looked back. // [I too don't know.] // As reports will have it // he's found in the coffee shop // the land of wandering ghosts // he goes there to see Mother // in her tight muumuu // smiling at his jokes // and the coffee attendant, // admires the smell of the hibiscus in Father's hands // in dead smiles // I saw Kate too // her thigh, stains of ugly permanent red fluids [the rapist was a careless painter] // curls had escaped at her memories and behind her ears // giving her a renaissance look // new friends // new plastic and rubber toys // Halloween masks // and Father, // he's in a pool of whipping flashes // from digital cameras // and cobwebs of the police // *"Police lines, do not cross"* // sprawling on withered hibiscus // and eventually, passing away // he does that trick // in his bath // whenever he had one. // I will cry and kiss him and sing dirges // and his skin, cold and papery against mine // will resurrect and request for a coffee rather than a coffin. // Please, women, milk your children // no autopsy is needed // no one is wanted // not even his mother that weaned him the day he was born // he skipped his prayer dose // *"although our days are numbered but may the Saviour come no time soon"* // and now, becomes a laboratory of *Pellicularia koleroga.*

Time Gossips

Reliable horologe – archaic hourglass,
sun's exit / the moon's august visit:

a patriarch crow seeks his morning crown,
pupil's aspiring sandals are quarter hands on
their neighbours' shoulders. They own quite
a prison-break architecture on used bean cake
papers – from bus stops' mobile shops.

Any woman protests daily,
exercising a right to hawk.
God's blessings are new every morning –
fingers outgrow the others daily.

Lost women are live soap operas, crooning
to family clothes' scrubs with blocks of bar soap.

Shaven science *tick and tock,*
cyclic mono-ads assumption(s).
Or maybe a mirror mime –

creativity could be deceitful. Anything could be art.
Cheek puffing – *"On my way* [...]"
Telephone's mouthpiece adultery – *"Come again* [...]"

An African Halloween witch – always tricked;
never treated. No outcry to change the stir of time.

Time gossips, she will surely tell.

More than Twelve Kind Words to a N*gga

We see black and white blend solely as a preset for photo manipulation.
If not mistaken, those are the only primary colours a Black boy could remember.

A Black man down my street never stops thinking
everything is a huge mistake. He recounts everyone makes a mistake;
even Oscar Wilde makes deliberate mistakes among his characters.
That of the cops' mistaken identity is not of colour-blindness but a
shark's inherent bloodthirstiness –
(*flash fiction with the same anticlimax of black ink spilled on the street sheet*).

To jog is to begin at the finish line of window-eyed audiences. To
memorize a nuclear dial is to illusion a young skunk creeping your
sidewalk – the genus you consider the most dangerous missile launching
in two legs, the healthy leper you think does not have a place in your
society. His pigment is a fitness watch beeping his steps, the
neighbourhood signboards are contestants for the fastest finger.

A Black mother is an Asian incubating grief swollen eyelid. A Black
father ages blind to the daily pulley of red and blue pills, he is the
forebear of the target his son inherits upon his back.

There are no visible signs of the angels of black death at work on the
highways. They lurk around with juxtaposed skin tones and grimy
garments. They are three-eyed monsters with a third on their body – the
same angels pray with a knee and cause a grown-up man to cry for his
mother's presence – their Messiah didn't teach them how to fish
without soaking their singlets, how to catch a fly without a clap sound
boomerang.

So, when the traffic light waves your feet to a clutch, such that the
highway melody messes up highlife and the breeze tunes ascendos
and crescendos around your shadow.
Run, Black boy. Run! Or please, don't move at all.
Pick one; this is no joke. Be decisive.

(M)easter

A young sot who knows no score piddles by God's acre with

Christ's presence at the threshold, waiting to hand him a gun and

say, "Come with me, young man ... to Galilee, and I'll take you

home for an everlasting piss."

First-Degree Murder

What – another brick of Jericho is connubial like divorce?

At the time, it seemed like time surged aback
the ancient Christ's counts as I scanned the
usual twelve disciples barcoding the jury box.

BC, the redolence of aloof feet, smoked gullet and moist
mouthparts jarred my torpor before the gavel rattled. I
remained an appendix of statutory looks, crippled by
academic paralegalism.

Abraham Unharmed!
Whom we expected walked in, sprouting grey strands on the
bark of his head – sour skin, while an infinity amulet coiled his
wrists. Volcanic murmurs ping-ponged acoustic ears. The calm
clerk advertised sealed lips with a life-large demonstration. All
took a vow of silence, and ovate flowers cramped sharply from
my abdomen.

Abraham! Oh, Abraham!! Suddenly amnesiac.
His forgotten friction ridges patterned forensic Sellotapes, whirlpooled
over the murder knife in his son's throat.
His defence: tap-like, ran out of essentially crammed judicial salivas.

His dandruff-fur wig itched his objections too curled to untangle.
Stand-taking, cripple-healed, Abraham's
oaths, hooked Adam's apple in his windpipe.

His divorced wife sat empty as a chipped jug, a torn
canvas in the court's gallery.
But what wealth had a man who lost his sweat, mind and son?
Silence and the air hung as curious blankets.
Acrimony and alimony were the plots against his matrimony.
He snorted like a bass singer, remoulding vibration into shatters of fragile listeners.
The case zipped on a blurry eye, and my journal, an archaic sheet.

AC, the police escorted him out like trafficking flies. Not even
the bailiff saw that I had an undue bleeding cascade in my
underwear that could've attracted the first-degree murder.
Though he rotated his surveillance eyes tirelessly.

BC – Before the case; AC – *After the case*

How to Jail a Bird

– or how to bail on your bed.

First, one needs a nose respirator or a lab coat, a
science student or a surgeon.

Lock the bird up in a box made up of transparent carpentry.
Fear is enough to make a bird a scapegoat, the sky is what a bird needs
to disappear.

Dissection into a correctional institution is an inside job.
The bird is not caged.

It would be best if you placed a penny in an inmate's hand.
The officer's circumrotation is from the right; you take a left.

The bird has a different look, maybe a butterfly – the one that flings
around your belly when you're called upon
to give a speech.

Something like a slingshot is us on you from the audience.
You're not sure; your mind is a battlefield of negativity.

The bird will not be caged.
Tonight, the correctional officers are not changing shifts.
The prison smells the same. When you wake from your bed, the dissection is your body structure
carving your likeness on a foam.

Your hands are in plain view all times; visitors are not allowed to hug
nor touch you.
You know this is not pure science, the deadliest weapon is launched in
your psyche.

A bird's cage is her song.

You're a survivor; you'll bring the war in your throat to its knees.

Please take out your cell apparatus, that item we use to put one within electronic frames.

Smile. Chirp. Break loose. Let the still-life victim escape.

Ventris Tui

after Frank O'Hara's "Ave Maria"

Uncle Sam's wives
              the house is stuffy   your stepchildren are sick of the house's motionless

pictures   and they underweight on many too many candies   let them walk their elephantine

bones down the street   so they won't catch you snoring during prayer hours

                     Isn't your worry what will become of their soul when they arrive
from the flicks produced and directed by a negro

                     But when you be over the hills as over the hills you shall be someday

they won't curse ya in vernacular   neither will they label you no goddamn terrorist like

Tupac's godmother   Daze of praises will shrine their thoughts   as they'll wash

                     mudslides off your hunchback dutifully   and grow successful

enough to journey beyond the western hemisphere to close business deals in silhouettes

of cyclorama puppetry   string dangles of handshakes exchanges   or Ave Maria

     they will call upon you   real quick   when they puke their first semen secretion

That way, they cost your pious image a speck of cream   or dark wine   for the church to see

     and bow in murmurs   because these kids don't get to find out for themselves the

differences between an incense smell and a popcorn's liquefying butter

Like when the lights are coming up on the audience's tears after a white-and-black clip stops

reeling closing credits, something drives younglings like them into the cars

of any cute stranger that can swear to be Christians but lives in a shared quarter far away

from San Antonio   Oh mothers   when last did you see this rugged smile on your

            nipper's face like when you sit at the entrance of the house like a bald (*chemo*) eagle,

    counting thirty-five stars flagging cerulean sky   and they return home reeling fresh

accents, recalling new friends' names and eye colours   after years of a more inclusive

        isolation denial   aging as souvenirs   now you are sure that they may pray for

your sin at the hour of death   but should you not listen   your recovering Caesarean

breasts will unthread   when you chance upon the kids with their laptops   flickering

            homemade silver sins   against their faces   as they pray to their wiggling hands

while Tupac's "Hail Mary" jams   loudly   in the disguise of their darker rooms

Omo Baba Kanto

for Ojeniyi Samson

The final paper untucked us as origami, sweat-mapped with
volatile future promises. Our knuckles snapped as plastic pens.

Buckled belts healed their poked holes. Shoelaces held out
wrapping arms for a shuffle of molecular embrace. By the smell

of their armpits, we could tell the hardworking ones. The
management let us mix in all flavour kinds of smiles refill. Still,

I somehow cared about the answer to the exam question no 8.
I however did the rest of the writing on my crush's white tee.

I confessed – her to be a train whose slightest motion swept me
off my black leather shoe. You, a mini vehicle, idled in front of

the head girl. Knowing well she's always the head boy's, you
believed in a chance slimmer than her skirt. As we talked beforehand,

about your cliché smell & poor comments; never to begin with
"Comment tu t'appelles." French's always accidental in your slippery

tongue. She found you funny & took you as a new crew to her neck.
You folded a three-dimensional heart, swelling a tortoise hunch from

heavy schoolbags hauled through the lagging academic years. I put
on a cheap Bluetooth speaker & it yelled Connection! like a drill

sergeant – as if to command you to get your shit together. It's a real-
life happening: that the following day, she might tell her friends she

hugged a flagpole. At ease, you tightened the English tie with which
you almost hung yourself. All back to base, you said her hairstyle

wasn't the problem, her forehead was. That way, you signed out a dry
joke: like thinking, disc jockeying was your way: not lacing ties in

imitation of a doctoral future. For what have we to prove to a bunch
of professing life experiences? Trying to cut deals in suit pant's sharp,

raw gators. Not kraaling into textbooks during on-spot questioning.
Nor inventing planes, boats, horses of question papers. Not dealing

with iron-stamped uniform & mufti sin. Nor getting ready for an
arranged marriage: not on one's mark to-a-go. Just to embrace the

stardom flex of autograph-generosity on bosoms with permanent markers.
Cloudburst & crowdburst; time for a share of the country's national tea made

with grotto-a-grotto pots of local routes leading home. Thunder snatched any
child seeking cover in the only mirror his father could afford. Trees steeped

confidential lessons of life as a flee-market & with forty leaves exercise books
upthrusted as umbrella miracles, "Crayfish multiplied. Remi remained an orphan

& Samson, a footballer. Goodbye, goodbye to Kanto's son," we marched.

VERONICA

Now a citizen of the world, wearing a feel always best
before October, living a western life, waving to say "hi"
to any polite passerby that waves back & mutters
a prayer that asks the Lord to make way for you.

The Westlife song playing on the radio stays non-static.

I weep every day for an avalanche to sweep me home.
Or drainage pipes. Black ice. Blue lights. On Halloween,
I wear an Elohim costume with print of Lagos on my chest.
Then I ask everyone to shoot me colour guns, camouflage lies,
flammable saliva or rubber bullets' casings. To aim a couple
more Shetani prayers or literally anything asshole of-a-rock.
No need to apologize for bothering me.

The Westlife song playing on the radio stays.

Surveyors take semi-seconds of the recess to spa their
aging limbs, to return winking well against viewfinders.
They have no future dream to leave uncaptured.
There are no pothole(s) in a dream tiled with your tongue.
An undercover police, without permit, parks by our front yard.
Kissing a chameleonic pet in hand, with his eyeballs in the nose.
The wind change styles as jazzy street riders' forthcoming brand
pageantry. Per kilometre, they owe the eye a true colour.

The Westlife song plays on the radio.

After your burial I went for a walk, my hands didn't swing.
I went missing in motion – like through a straightforward
route which didn't look the same on the way back.
Then your two left-eyed friend cringing peppers with
a rock, saw me & redressed her wrapper to ask me to take
heart as if a free drink from the refrigerator in her retail shop.
Here, women collect their first sons from their yards' hangers
through the avalanche of orphan heirs icing in back seats.

The Westlife song plays & –
A line is left static, intentionally

My left palm pavements are environmentally approved permeable(s),
saving your scripted garden from flooding every fall.

I'm glad you poured some prayers into my palm: you trusted I would hold
on to them like your bank statement(s) postmen deliver home every month.

You can still trust this route home, Veronica.

Who Is Avalanche?

more like general labourers' mock trial of "Where from
or for how long being here?" not so different from the

general question of "Who is your father in this land?" &
when asked, i play into the corners of spectating eyeballs

in search of pity nod, but it's a first step to keeping one's
boots lighter. a crow clocks in a minute late or so in my

head: for the city, if not only me, falls behind its hustle
schedule. i mean since i left home, i have been living in

my head or more realistically, my high-mileage Chevrolet
that makes the nearest coffee shop a migrant's life journey.

at least, the morning bus athlete cup has passed me over
& every stop's a little closer. no familiar lateness will find

me in the vehicle that stops at every railway crossing, like
a schoolboy caught & factorized at an early age. young

drivers perform civic duties, sweeping stunts under their
parents' unaccord season tires. cross-guards pray for Christ

to come this time around while the municipal speed cameras are
coming soon. my toes are heavy-duty wheel locked. my mother's

voicemails are pleas not to forget my promises, for the family's
breadwinner has been sacked from the bakery back home, where

a bike man could shoot me through this time. with my body count
equalling the pedestrian's crosswalks countdown, the thunder god

in the red light camera refuses to print an immediate picture. i look
in the rear-view for the sin a foreigner doesn't inherit from his fore-

father: ghost wailing from back seat. the sky's orange yoke drops
by my side mirror like the city's melting pot. layered up like a

weather lawyer, the cold caught proves a scapegoat doubt for the
day. how best to trim a skin tag jacket bulge, is being stuck at

a Pain & Flinch intersection when the day isn't so traffic terrific.
blank chuckle & tooth implant accent: straight-piped lips & winter-

glued saliva, "who is avalanche?" an after-lunch taste or audition
callback for the same role with coloured scenarios. a backup &

devilish small comment – that if were the one, i wouldn't let a cliché
pet bird go scot-free. i'll call off whatever is due the following day

like a clarion call with an unknown number, just to rewatch it trying
to fit its jaws through the hooks of songs of freedom & survival.

waiting on the return of consumers / workers / students / loans /
taxes, to proof fluency of debt to death.

Gills

since I last saw a corkscrew
pop a gaseous cache,

self-split broilers had saluted a handful
of worms neglected eggshells, finely.

per day, a newborn is found paddling the
river by the mountainside. river snakes bade

yo-yo dolls in springy bellies: with nerve-tip
umbilical(s); ready to hiss, shed or spit grief.

mothers wipe clean the lantern-glassed earth
with tears, without drenching its short-lived wick.

proof-solution for separating dust from soul from water from
kerosene. the last smoker mourner licks a tribunal tribute:

of returning home with dull headlight & cigarette trafficator,
paper bills of health & death. balance carried down:

fizzing the maws of disrespectful fishes,
Mr. Titus has always been a sweet man.

卌 卌 卌 卌 卌 卌
卌 卌 卌 卌 卌 卌
卌 卌 ||

AcKnowLedgEmeNTS

I want to acknowledge *African Writer Magazine* for publishing an earlier draft of "Asylum and Coffee Shop," *Shallow Tales Review* for "Ad Lib," *Kalahari Review* for "Here or to Go," *The Medium* (University of Toronto Mississauga) for "Fig. 1.2 Black Skin Diagram" and "Rap Sheet," *Beyond Words* for "Styling Pik," *Guesthouse* for "Fallen Walls, Mere Floating Portions," *Ampersand Review* for "Encore" and "Wait a Sec," *Words Rhymes & Rhythms* for "Not Every Father Leaves" and "Window-Shopping," *Barren Magazine* for "Pear Trees Hanging Minor Negroes in Tie," Stone of Madness Press for "Migraine Thesis," *Windsor Review* for "Driving Test," Britta B's Open Drawer Contest for "More Than Twelve Kind Words to a N*gga," Awards London for "First-Degree Murder," Poets in Nigeria for "Terpsichore" and "(M)easter" and Kreative Diadem on which "How to Jail a Bird" and "I Know" first appeared.

Thanks to Mr. Ibiyemi Kayode, my high school literature teacher, whose first saw the laureate in me.

Thanks to Adìo, Segun Michael and Ngaju Micheal for introducing me to poetry.

Thanks to Dr. Soji Cole, Prof. Geoffrey and Brent Wood.

Thanks to Kudirat, who I am her life's largest poop.

Thanks to Dada, of whose night shift I am today.

Thanks to Paul who found me halfway many-a-writer's bin, piecing & / recycling for the sake of our literary climate.

Thanks to those who help pick up my accent's diacritics that fall off when I English.

Thanks to the theatre's backstage safekeeping my secrets.

Thanks to my foreign friends who could for once actually pronounce my name rightly.

Thanks to the clarion always calling to apologize for making me a stray little slug. I might consider making this a dropped cartridge-like case when I hit my target.

Thanks to our lead actors whose voices are hapless migrants sinking the orchestra pit.

Thanks to those who, out of love and in attempts to light my cake, burnt it.

Thanks to the Canadians that I accidentally hit their cars from behind and woke up the next day to ask if was feeling alright.

Thanks to the Blue and Christmas lights that cured my epilepsy.

Thanks to the foreign lady that took me in her vacant brain cell.

Thanks to the maple leaf that fell on my head on my graduation day.

Thanks to tow trucks' halogen lights that helped me see tomorrow last night.

Thanks to the Bayowas, Alao Toyyib, Claire, Phingo and Sultan for reading and never understanding my poems.

AYOMIDE BAYOWA is an award-winning Nigerian Canadian poet, actor and film-maker. He holds a BA in Theatre and Creative Writing from the University of Toronto and is the (2021–24) poet laureate of Mississauga, Ontario, Canada. He is a top-ten gold entrant of the 9th Open Eurasian Literary Festival and Book Forum, UK, a finalist of the Frontier Poetry Global Poetry Prize and was long-listed for both the UnSerious Collective Fellowship and 2021 *Adroit Journal* Poetry Prize. He won first place in the 2020 July Open Drawer Poetry Contest, the June/July 2021 edition of the bimonthly Brigitte Poirson Poetry Contest (BPPC) and second place in the 2021 K. Valerie Connor Poetry Contest's Student Category. He has appeared in a long list of literary magazines, including *Windsor Review*, *Kalahari Review*, IceFloe Press, *Barren Magazine*, *Agbowó*, *Guesthouse*, *Stone of Madness Press*, *Ampersand Review*, *Tipton Poetry Journal*, *The Offing* and *Beyond Words Literary Magazine*. He is the editor-in-chief of *Echelon Poetry* and currently reads poetry for *Adroit Journal*.